How To Stop Feeling Ashamed and Guilty

Step By Step Comprehensive Guide on How to Stop Feeling Guilty and Ashamed Over Everything

Introduction

Have you struggled with guilt and shame for as long as you can remember? In that, you often apologize and try to make amends when you recognize that you're wrong, but even then, the guilt and shame hang around you like a bad smell.

And,

Have you tried everything to break the negative cycle of shame and guilt to no avail? And what is more, is your guilt and shame sometimes so acute that you cannot muster enough courage and confidence to apologize and seek a way forward? And as much as your heart desires and aches for you to be on good terms with everyone, do you stay put, allowing your shame to gnaw at you mercilessly?

More importantly,

Are you determined to kill your shame before it kills your self-esteem?

Are you tired of viewing yourself and your character in a perennially negative light owing to your chronic shame?

Do you know you're being irrational and unfair to yourself when you do this, but your shame keeps propping up negative thoughts and self-perceptions?

And,

Have you wanted to stop this habit for the longest time but don't know how?

If you've answered YES, this guide is here for you!

We'll break down guilt and shame and their productive and toxic variants and show you precisely how to kill your shame.

More interestingly,

We'll do it directly, efficiently, and practically so you'll have every tool to kill your shame and guilt and build yourself back up.

So, let's get started!

PS: I'd like your feedback. If you are happy with this book, please leave a review on Amazon.

Please leave a review for this book on Amazon by visiting the page below:

https://amzn.to/2VMR5qr

Table of Contents

Chapter 1: Understanding Shame And Guilt – How Do They Compare & Relate To Each Other?

To defeat your enemy, you must first know him. And so, it follows that the first step to understanding how to stop feeling ashamed and guilty is to understand what both terms mean and their fundamental differences.

We often use the words "guilt" and "shame" interchangeably. They both refer to a negative/lousy emotion or feeling resulting from our adverse actions. However, while they are similar in many ways and founded on the same salient things, they also mean entirely different things.

This chapter will greatly emphasize the differences and distinctions between guilt and shame. Both emotions significantly affect how we see ourselves, others, and the world. As such, we must thoroughly define them and their differences so that we have an excellent base on which to build this guide on.

Shame vs. Guilt – Comparing and Contrasting the Two Emotions

According to psychologists, **guilt** is *a default emotional condition that occurs when you believe you have fallen short of maintaining the moral standards of others or yourself.* Like shame, guilt brings thoughts of our failures and unpleasant emotions like grief, rage, or anxiety. Guilt may be beneficial, but only if you deliberately regulate it on your part and do not allow it to run amok and dominate your every thought.

Shame, in contrast, is characterized *as a strong negative emotion about yourself that results from falling short of your own or other people's expectations.*

Sounds similar to guilt, no?

The primary distinction between guilt and shame is that while the former is likely beneficial (albeit in small doses), the latter, if not promptly checked, will poison your mindset and lead you to believe that you're genuinely the worst person prone to screwing up. Shame is detrimental since it eventually results in a loss of self-esteem, mainly if it isn't addressed.

They are equally unpleasant – this is true – but shame is like guilt's evil twin.

Let's examine a case in point.

You mistakenly ran a red light because, in your hurry, you failed to see the light changing to yellow, almost hitting another driver in the process. If you feel the usual, non-toxic guilt (more on toxic and non-toxic shame and guilt in the next chapter), you will likely say, *"Oh my God, I bungled that up so badly. I should practice more caution. I should stay focused on these roads and save myself and others unnecessary grief."*

On the other hand, shame is a lot more toxic and damaging to your self-esteem. Shame will push you to say, *"I'm such a bad driver, man. I'm a dreadful person. I shouldn't be permitted to drive a vehicle."*

Do you see the stark difference between both responses?

Unlike guilt, shame (unfairly and irrationally) attacks who you are as an individual, not what you did. Shame may also spawn from outside of yourself – including from folks who do not know you – making its deconstruction of your self-esteem and self-perception even more unfair and irrational.

For instance, if the driver you almost hit when you ran the red light lambasted you and called you a horrible person, shame can cause you to irrationally latch onto their nasty comments and perceive them to be true.

The distinction between guilt and shame is quite significant, all being said. *Guilt is beneficial when not allowed to run amok, enabling us to recognize and alter potentially harmful behavior.* On the other hand, *shame attacks your character and self-perception* rather than the behavior and finds fault with your being, which is unfair and not beneficial in any way or form.

Everyone experiences shame and guilt, though some more than others. However, you can learn to manage emotions with the right tips and strategies.

How To Stop Being Ashamed and Guilty

Behaviors, Actions, and Possessions concerning Shame and Guilt

Unlike shame, **guilt** is typically *connected to possessions, actions, and behaviors.* You feel guilty when you hurt somebody or are not proud of your actions or words. You are aware that what you do may cause others to feel emotionally or physically bad, and since you care about them, you feel awful about what you did and wish to make amends.

As we get older, we could also experience guilt for having things others don't have. This is the constructive aspect of guilt, provided our feelings of guilt are managed and not allowed to be over the top.

On the other hand, **shame** seldom *has much to do with our behaviors and actions.* Yes, you might experience shame when you do things you or others deem wrong, but on a more

Page | 14

profound level, the emotion isn't related to our deeds. It mostly has to do with ourselves.

When we feel shame; we may have acted inappropriately, but instead of reflecting on our behavior; we focus on what we perceive it to mean—we believe it to be evidence that we are a nasty, foolish, inadequate, or selfish person. And owing to this, shame, unlike guilt, has zero benefits. It's detrimental to who we are and our evolution as parents, siblings, friends, romantic partners, etc.

The Connection between Shame and Guilt

We know shame and guilt are anchored in the same actions and behaviors.

But is there a more profound connection between both?

The answer is yes.

When **guilt goes unchecked**, and you allow it to dominate your thoughts and influence your actions for far too long, **it becomes toxic guilt**, which then swiftly and steadily **transmutes into shame.**

That is why checking your guilt before it goes too far is essential. You must learn to tell yourself, *"Hey, I may have messed up, but it was an honest mistake, and I know I have the mettle to do better in the future."*

Why?

If you allow your guilt to morph into toxic guilt and finally shame/toxic shame, you may find yourself saying things like, *"I'm a horrible person who does not deserve anything good,"* and other irrational things.

A Negative Self-Evaluation Is Never Necessary

If you are familiar with guilt (which you very likely are), you know that making a mistake that hurts others also hurts you. You may occasionally do something hurtful that leaves you feeling guilty enough to want to atone and make amends soonest possible.

Having the awareness that you erred and that it may be necessary to make amends is, by and large, beneficial. For instance, just because you knowingly took a little extra change than was owed to you from the cashier doesn't mean you're a terrible person. It simply means that you took a singular action that may go against your or the societal principles.

When you experience non-toxic guilt rather than toxic guilt and shame, you stop seeing your occasional mistakes as a part of who you are. You can still change and rectify the situation when you do wrong since you are still a good person.

In essence, **all of us occasionally make mistakes**. Accepting this reality is healthy because mistakes are part and parcel of being human. Overwhelming guilt will swiftly transform into shame, as we've pointed out. However, managing your guilt in healthy ways rather than allowing it to get out of hand could have some incredibly positive effects on you.

To wrap up,

Making the distinction between guilt and shame will help you to manage your emotions better.

Remember,

We all make mistakes, no matter how grave; making one or three doesn't have to put dents in your self-esteem. Instead, you can evolve, grow from your experience, and learn from your guilt.

But,

You must keep it checked, so it doesn't take a toxic tang and spill over into shame.

However, unfortunately, far too many of us have allowed our feelings of guilt and shame to dominate us and go unchecked for too long.

But the good news is that this guide will help you manage your toxic guilt and shame and break out of prison for good.

Let's learn more in the next chapter!

Chapter 2: What Is The Difference Between Normal/Productive Guilt Versus Toxic/Unproductive Guilt And Shame

Chapter 1 compared and contrasted shame and guilt in depth and established the connection between both. We found that if you control guilt and do not allow it to seep in too deeply, it will likely be beneficial since it fixates on the behavior or set of actions, allowing us to improve. Shame, however, fixates on your character and self-perception – often irrationally and unfairly – gradually eroding your self-esteem.

We also established that guilt, when allowed to set in and dig its claws in for far too long, develops into toxic guilt and, ultimately, shame.

Toxic guilt and shame *invite resentment, self-disgust, and other unfavorable emotions.* It can creep into your thoughts like lethal cyanide, trapping you in a torturous cycle of negative self-talk and slowly killing your self-esteem and sense of self. As a result, you may feel unimportant and small, even as an adult who knows very well that they're not insignificant.

Everyone sometimes feels guilt and even shame, although some experience them more often or deeply than others.

Guilt often has a cultural basis. It reiterates the thought that some actions might harm others and harm society; it can support social norms and uphold a well-balanced, fair culture. You may feel guilty if you engage in these potentially dangerous behaviors and actions or even have thoughts about them.

But at what point does usual – even productive – guilt turn toxic and ultimately develop into shame? It isn't easy.

• How Do Toxic Guilt and Shame Differ from Normal/Productive Guilt?

The following salient characteristics will help you determine if your guilt has dug its heels in too long and morphed into toxic guilt and, ultimately, shame:

- It causes you to doubt your value or feel worthless.

- You have issues properly recognizing and addressing your emotions, owing to your conditioning to feel that your feelings are shameful.

- You often feel anxiety and despair.

- You view situations in terms of *"I am a bad person"* rather than *"I did something bad."*

- You have a constant stream of negative internal dialogue.

- You'll try to avoid further embarrassment and shame, even if it means putting yourself in unfair and unfavorable conditions.

• The Roots of Toxic Guilt and Shame

A lot of the time, chronic toxic guilt and shame *stem from one's formative years*. In other words, the seed of shame is planted when you are younger – usually as kids dependent on your parents/caregivers, teachers, etc.

Some of the root causes of toxic guilt and shame are:

- ✓ Neglect or abuse on a verbal, physical, or emotional level

- ✓ Having had caregivers who struggled with mental illness.

- ✓ Being in a situation where domestic violence of any type is taking place, as kids.

- ✓ Traumatizing events in childhood, such as a loss of a dear one.

- ✓ Emotionally unavailable Caregivers.

- ✓ Unaddressed mental health conditions when young, like anxiety or depression.

- ✓ Being gaslighted constantly as children.

As a child, it's easy to believe that your value is heavily influenced by outside factors rather than your inner grit, owing to constant unfavorable feedback from teachers, parents, or other adults. Even though it's an absurd way of thought as an adult, you probably didn't know any better as a child.

And what's more – we rely heavily on our parents, caregivers, teachers, sports coaches, etc., when young because they have authority over us. So, when they have something negative to say about us, it's difficult for our child brains to process the information correctly. That's especially true if it was dispensed irresponsibly and in a toxic, unconstructive manner by unhealthy and emotionally irresponsible adults.

When we are young, we lack a lot of cognitive finesse. We ***don't possess the logical maturation*** at that age to say to ourselves, *"Well, while my parents or professors are right in reprimanding me, it was honestly an honest mistake on my part. I need to improve, but this is not the biggest deal."*

Also,

We **lack the cognitive prowess and experience** to weave the fabric of logic like this. Instead, we tend to carry our guilt, which hits us heavily. And suppose you had the misfortune of growing up in a toxic household with many put-downs, snark, and emotional detachment. In that case, your guilt can flow freely and eventually transmute to toxic guilt and shame.

As a result, you may have begun to doubt your worth at a very young age and used unhealthy coping mechanisms to cope with internalized shame, some of which may have seeped into adulthood.

What's the downside of this?

Adults suffering from toxic guilt and shame **frequently have trouble forming genuine bonds and friendships**. Unfortunately, we may struggle with *low self-esteem and feelings of inadequacy*, even when we're talented, kind, and fabulous individuals at our core, which puts us at risk for self-harm and depression.

Also, we may ***crave other folks' approval*** far too much, which increases our propensity to engage in unhealthy relationships.

Here s how and why:

Why Toxic Guilt and Shame are a Big Deal

You're likely to internalize negative messages and comments about your personality or intellect if you consistently or constantly heard them as a child. And while this is an entirely natural response, it is nevertheless very detrimental.

Why?

You will carry forth a false sense of your unworthiness rather than momentarily feeling guilty and ashamed of your poor decisions and promptly learning from them. Particularly throughout childhood, when you are still developing your sense of self, this shame may become ingrained in you, significantly distorting your perception of yourself and poisoning your internal dialogue, making it overly harmful and toxic.

Developing a healthy sense of self-worth will be challenging if you believe you're evil, unlovable, ignorant, and a host of other unfavorable and untrue things. Toxic guilt and shame will block any positive self-perception from developing. It is easy to view these as unchangeable permanent conditions, making it hard to move through life confidently and happily.

Here are several more negative effects of toxic guilt and shame:

1. It Isolates You

Negative self-talk resulting from toxic guilt and shame can cause you to withdraw and avoid social situations. You may have anxiety while discussing your "true" self with others owing to the erroneous belief that you are unworthy of their friendship or intimacy.

Incidences of infidelity or dishonesty are some examples of hurtful and regrettable actions likely related to toxic shame. Suppose you were dishonest or unfaithful in the past. In that case, you may feel that you do not deserve another opportunity or that you'll ruin anyone with whom you try to build a relationship, even after you've done everything possible to make amends.

2. It Leads to Distressing Emotions

Undesirable emotions like rage toward oneself and others may be triggered by negative self-talk that typically stems from shame. The same goes for other emotions like anxiety, dread, concern, sadness, and embarrassment.

Perfectionism can likely be fueled by toxic shame, leading to anxiety, dread, sadness, etc., because it's impossible to be perfect and not slip up occasionally.

3. Your Relationships are Negatively Impacted

It may be challenging to be vulnerable with people when you live with toxic guilt and shame. You may likely assume that if people discover how 'bad' or 'unworthy' you are, they'll distance themselves from you. As a result, you may hold back a lot about yourself and never be at ease letting down your guard around others, especially around your loved ones.

This may make you appear aloof and distant, making it difficult for others, your loved ones included, to trust you since they may think you are hiding something.

Toxic guilt and shame can also exacerbate problems in relationships. Even warm or sympathetic comments touching on some mistake you made or constructive criticism about your behavior can trigger memories of being shamed as a child and confirm feelings of personal inadequacy.

This inability to take constructive criticism in stride could make you overly defensive, angry, or depressed and cause you to either needlessly lash out at your partner/friends/loved ones/colleagues or emotionally withdraw and unfairly stonewall them.

4. It results in Negative, Self-Destructive Actions, and Behavior

Some of us, unfortunately, dip into unhealthy coping mechanisms to dull the mental and emotional ravages that toxic shame brings.

And,

In a misguided attempt at reclaiming control over our lives and cleaving away at the vice grip that shame has on our psyches, we may fall into unhealthy ways such as abusing substances, inflicting physical harm on ourselves, or developing disordered eating patterns.

These coping mechanisms may provide some momentary solace, but they don't address the toxicity brewing in us. As such, we end up doing more long-term damage to ourselves.

The Bottom Line

Although toxic shame often leaves deep mental and emotional wounds that can take a long time to heal, self-love and self-compassion, among other positive things, are effective remedies for curing the scars it leaves behind. This guide will do a thorough job of exploring the remedies for toxic guilt and shame.

Chapter 3: Identifying and Clarifying Your Guilt

You've undoubtedly done a few things you feel guilty about; we all have.

After all, mistakes and missteps are standard components of human development. Feeling guilty and ashamed about your mistakes is normal too. However, allowing the guilt to linger too long and turn into toxic guilt and shame can (and will) lead to physical and emotional distress.

Let's back up for a second and address something first:

Guilt has enormous power as an Emotion

You can improve your behavior and actions by acknowledging your mistakes and using guilt as an incentive. Doing so will help you better recognize what you may have gone about differently due to guilt.

But as we've already discussed, your guilt will become outright negative if allowed to fester for too long. To prevent this from happening, or – if it's already happened – put an emphatic stop to your toxic guilt and shame, you must first identify and clarify exactly what you feel guilty and ashamed of.

They say that a problem discussed is a problem half-solved. This chapter will arm you with information and tips on shining a light on the things you are guilty and ashamed of, and thus being able to unpack them and determine if they are worth the crippling guilt and shame you feel over them.

Steps to Identifying and Clarifying Your Guilt

There are three steps to identifying and clarifying your guilt/source of guilt:

1) Acknowledging and Naming Your Guilt

The first step in identifying and defining what you are guilty and ashamed of is to "name your guilt."

We often make the mistake of trying our hardest to ignore, suppress or push aside our guilt. It often seems like a wise course of action to take. After all, if we do not think about it, it will gradually diminish and vanish. Right?

Wrong; in fact, the opposite is true.

Ignoring or suppressing your guilt may temporarily stop it from permeating your daily life, but hiding your feelings rarely serves as a long-term solution. It would help first to acknowledge your feelings and where they stem from, however awful and unpleasant it is for you, to conquer them truly.

But how?

Here is a simple exercise to help you acknowledge and name your guilt:

- ✓ Make time for yourself and find a quiet and private place.

- ✓ Have a small notebook or journal with you to write down your thoughts.

- ✓ Ponder what you feel guilty of, say it aloud, and then write it down. For instance, "I feel guilty and ashamed because I yelled at my kids," "I did not fulfill my promise to my lovely coworker," or "I cheated on my test."

✓ Be as specific as possible. Keep your descriptions straightforward, and write down all the exact reasons you can find. Once you have a proper perspective on where your guilt and shame stem from, you get closer to conquering them.

2) Determining Your Guilt Type for Even Greater Clarity

There are four kinds of guilt. Some of us alternate between each category during our lives. Others may experience one or even more types of guilt concurrently.

Therefore, you must assess your guilt after acknowledging and naming it to determine its category.

But before we define and specify the four kinds of guilt, why is it essential to know where your guilt falls?

Well, the answer to this is quite simple – remember what we said in the first sentence of the first chapter of this guide? To beat thy enemy, you must first know your enemy.

So,

✓ Once you clearly understand what kind(s) of guilt you are grappling with, you will be able to wield the right mental tools to deconstruct this guilt.

✓ You will also be able to refine the tips, strategies, and methods outlined in this guide to tackle your specific kind of guilt.

✓ Moreover, you will be in an even better position to verify and validate the source(s) of your guilt.

Here are the four kinds of guilt:

1) **Natural guilt**: We've discussed this one already; hence we won't unpack it too much. Simply put, natural guilt is the emotion you

experience after you believe you have made a mistake. For example, if you promised something and fell short, you might feel guilty and wish to apologize. Natural guilt is transient and disappears after settlement.

2) **Chronic guilt**: This kind of guilt develops due to ongoing stress and tension in your life over a considerable time. This stress/tension negatively impacts your behavior and interactions with others, making you feel guilty and ashamed. For instance, suppose you are a teacher who feels overworked and emotionally spent, which has likely affected your psyche for a while. In such a case, the ongoing stress and overwhelmedness can impact your interactions with your students over a long period, which can then cause you to feel guilty and ashamed.

3) **Collective guilt**: This kind of guilt involves a feeling of shared or community responsibility. For instance, collective guilt among city dwellers with apartments/houses of their own over those homeless in their area is possible. In this example, you, your neighbors, and fellow residents may experience guilt because you feel you have not done enough to assist. Since collective guilt is ingrained in systemic issues, it is more challenging to address.

4) **Survivor guilt**: Feelings of guilt and shame can result from witnessing and surviving traumatic experiences and knowing others were not so lucky. For instance, you may have survived an accident and now feel guilty for those less fortunate than you were. You may also feel guilty for having had considerable success when your close friends struggle to grow.

Undoubtedly,

Most of your reasons for feeling guilty will fall into either natural or chronic guilt.

However, you must thoroughly vet the reasons you wrote down and determine which category your guilt falls into.

3).Validating the Source

You need to validate the source of your guilt before you can truly address it.

Let's elaborate some more:

It's perfectly normal to feel guilty after doing something you know to be harmful or wrong. However, guilt can also sometimes develop in response to circumstances you had little to do with or little to no power over.

Therefore,

Determining if you are unjustifiably blaming yourself for circumstances beyond your control is crucial.

Unfortunately, far too many of us do this to ourselves, which makes it so much easier for our guilt to spiral into toxic guilt and shame. You may, for instance, feel bad for ending a relationship you knew was very toxic because your ex still loves you and is having difficulty moving on. Or you may feel guilty because you've got a great career while your best friend can't find meaningful employment.

We may also feel guilty because we feel that we have fallen short of the standards that we or others have set for us, regardless of how reasonable these standards are. The problem with this is that this guilt often fails to accurately reflect the effort and work you've made to try and get beyond the obstacles that stood in the way of accomplishing those objectives.

As such, you need to validate the source of your guilt and determine if it is valid or if you're simply being unfair to yourself, and that trauma you may have experienced in your formative years may be the foundation for the guilt and shame you feel.

Once you've identified, clarified, and validated your guilt; you're ready to attack and erase it from your psyche.

Chapter 4: Make Amends with Yourself and Anyone You May Have Hurt

"True confession – a really genuine confession that comes from the heart; often consists of talking about our deed(s) in a way that the soul is transformed in the process of telling it."
— Maude Petre

You probably hear a lot about how critical it is to forgive folks who harm you.

But what about forgiving ourselves? Isn't that just as important as well?

The answer is yes.

It is perfectly normal – even healthy – to have feelings of guilt about hurting someone; to feel remorse and regret; to wish that we could take it all back, and to have a pressing urge to do everything we can to make them feel better.

What is unhealthy, however, is to constantly criticize yourself for your mistakes and wrongs and conclude that you are a horrible person due to it.

We've already discussed the distinctions and linkage between guilt and shame, so we won't belabor the point any further, as you already know how they compare and how guilt, if unchecked, morphs into toxic guilt and then shame.

This chapter will look at **making amends with yourself and those you may have wronged** to directly attack your lingering guilt and shame and push them out of your psyche.

So how do you do that?

Making amends with others is, by and large, a straightforward thing. What isn't so direct is making amends with yourself and forgiving yourself.

As such, this chapter will go deep into making amends with yourself and then round out with making amends with others.

Forgiving Yourself May be Hard; very Hard Indeed

The most challenging thing you'll probably ever get to do/navigate to overcome your shame and guilt will likely be forgiving and making amends for ways you've harmed or hurt others.

In fact,

It might be the most challenging thing you'll ever have to accomplish. This is particularly true if you've perpetuated the abuse cycle stemming from trauma and abuse in your childhood years by inflicting pain on someone else in the same manner you were mistreated.

Here is an example of why making amends with yourself may be the hardest thing you'll ever do:

If you suffered abuse and trauma as a child, you know firsthand the harm that child abuse causes to a child. And you are personally aware of the devastating effects abuse's associated shame may have on someone's life. And as such, forgiving yourself for mistreating/abusing a child could be challenging.

Dr. Kim Rahul Ambani is a world-class counselor and psycho-analyst. Here are a few accounts of what his patients have expressed of themselves to him about their feelings of guilt and shame:

- "I know how much it hurt me when my dad hit me. And yet I have done the same things to my very own kids, whom I love to death. It's unacceptable, and I feel I do not deserve forgiveness."

- "As a child, it crushed my heart when someone made a promise to me, and I waited eagerly, only for them not to deliver. I still have vivid memories of my disappointment as a kid. And yet here I am doing the same thing, making promises I know I won't fulfill and knowing how disappointed the other person will likely be."

- "I feel like an irredeemable monster. I'm at a loss for words because I am ashamed of mistreating my staff. Coming up the ranks, I was devastated every time one of my managers walked all over me, yelled at me, or diminished my efforts. But I have become the person I used to loathe, and I feel so guilty and ashamed of what I have become."

Looking at it this way, it becomes apparent that forgiving yourself may not be as easy as you thought. As such, you must do it tactfully and keep an open mind.

The 3 Routes Toward Self-Forgiveness

It may seem challenging to forgive and make amends with yourself for the harm you may have done to others, particularly those you care about and love. But it is doable. The three main effective ways that you can go about it are:

✓ Self-understanding.

✓ Common humanity.

✓ Earning your forgiveness: pushing yourself to take full responsibility, making the necessary apologies, and promptly making amends.

1. Self-Understanding

You must develop self-understanding to arrive at self-forgiveness, notably if you experienced abuse as a kid and continued the abuse cycle with your kids.

Forgiving yourself for any/all ways that you have harmed others will be easier to do once you understand that the particular trauma(s) that you suffered caused issues within you that was beyond your control.

For instance, suppose your addiction(s) have caused you to hurt your loved ones. If you feel guilty about it, understand that the habit, whether to drugs, alcohol, shopping, food, sex, or gambling, has just been a coping mechanism for anxiety and stress that may stem back to your childhood.

But why should you develop this understanding?

It will be easier to stop bashing yourself for your abusive ways once you understand that being abused as a child is why you started being offensive to your partner, lovely kids, or others or established an unhealthy pattern of enabling abusers.

However, this is not to say you do not take responsibility for your wrongs. More than ever, you need to take full accountability for your wrongs to practice self-forgiveness. But understand that there is more to the story and that you're not an irredeemable monster.

2. Common Humanity and Steadily Developing Self-Compassion

Kristin Neff, an associate professor of human developmental dynamics at the University of Texas at Austin, has done numerous comprehensive studies on self-compassion.

She identifies acknowledging the shared human experience, or what she refers to as "Common Humanity," as an essential component of self-compassion. She says, *"Self-compassion recognizes that all people are imperfect and that making poor decisions and experiencing guilt for them is unavoidable."*

Everyone has, in reality, negatively impacted, at the very least, one other individual in ways that have influenced that person's life. All of us are guilty of it.

However, knowing this and understanding that you aren't alone will:

✓ Make it easier for you to forgive and show yourself some compassion.

✓ It will also free you from the self-loathing that makes it so hard to forgive yourself and allow you to address and respond to the situation or circumstance differently. Empathy and compassion for your genuine suffering and the suffering of others you have harmed may help you gain the insight to think of and develop ways to aid those you've hurt rather than torturing yourself with endless shame and guilt.

Here's a simple exercise to do:

- Draw up a list of everyone you've hurt and how you've hurt them. Review each name, noting all the factors and circumstances that contributed to your actions or inaction. Compare your harmful deeds and words with any abuse or neglect you may have experienced. Now consider other initiating elements like a familial addiction history or perhaps one of violence, along with other factors such as stress brought on by monetary or marital issues.

- Now, ask yourself why you may have done the things you did. Was your anger, for instance, so overwhelming that you could not contain it? Have you been conditioned to loathe/undervalue yourself so much that paying attention to how hurtful you were to others was difficult? Had you erected such a solid defensive barrier that you could not feel sympathy or self-compassion – at least at the moment – for the victim of your actions?

- Now that you know the circumstances and factors that influenced your behavior try applying Common Humanity's ethos to yourself. Yes, you were a flawed, fallible person who occasionally acted in a way that harmed others, just like everyone else. So, recognize and accept your imperfections as human limitations. Allow yourself to feel sympathy for yourself. Be kind to yourself.

3. Earning Your Forgiveness

If you still have trouble forgiving yourself, ask yourself, "Why would I not want to forgive myself?". If your answer is, "I do not deserve it," if you still think you do not deserve compassion, then perhaps you believe you have to earn it. And this is alright too.

How do you go about earning your forgiveness?

You **must first own your wrongdoings** to both yourself and other people. You may not believe you deserve forgiveness unless you are completely honest about how you've hurt others, first to yourself, then to that person, or those you've hurt (if feasible). And incidentally, they might not be too willing to extend their forgiveness to you unless you admit to what you did to hurt the person or individuals you have wronged.

Nobody benefits when you wallow too long in your errors, not even the person you wronged.

When you immediately accept responsibility for your hurtful actions and set about trying to earn your forgiveness, you may at first feel more guilty and ashamed. However, that guilt and shame will soon be replaced by a sense of self-respect and sincere pride.

Here's how to go about earning your forgiveness:

✓ Spend considerable time pondering how your actions (or inaction) have hurt the other person. Completing the sentence below may help:

"I   hurt

_____by_____."

✓ Make sure to have in writing all the ways that your actions or lack of hurt this person.

"I caused _____to suffer in these ways_____."

✓ The next stage is approaching the people you harmed and apologizing for what you've done. It's crucial to let those you've wronged know they've got every right to be angry and to urge them to express it to you directly. Nevertheless, ensure you don't let anyone humiliate or verbally assault you. The goal is to make them understand that you acknowledge your wrongs and have enough respect for them and yourself to seek their forgiveness.

Here's more on seeking forgiveness from others and making amends with them:

Apologizing to Others

The impact of your admission of what you did to hurt others increases if you offer an honest, heartfelt apology.

And,

Often, many folks who suffered childhood abuse express their desire for the abuser to acknowledge their wrongdoing and extend an apology to them.

Think back to a time when you believed someone had wronged you. What did you require from that particular person for you to be able to forgive them?

An apology, no?

But most of us also need more than just the phrase *"I'm sorry."* We need the perpetrator to accept responsibility for their actions and demonstrate remorse or regret for harming us.

*A **sincere apology*** to someone you've harmed will go a long way in erasing your guilt and shame. On the other hand; if you don't feel enough remorse after hurting somebody else but extend a heartfelt apology to them; this will serve as a helpful reminder: when we have to apologize to somebody, the default emotion in our psyches is ashamed.

So, the next time you're tempted to repeat the very same action you apologized for, keeping the shame you felt when apologizing in mind can help you resist the urge and take a different course of action.

Our self-confidence, self-esteem, and overall view on life may all be impacted by our level of self-respect. We gain a strong sense of respect and regard for ourselves when we have the mettle to own our mistakes, overcome our differences and concerns, and humble ourselves enough to apologize. By apologizing, you're essentially saying, *'I respect you, and I'm demonstrating to you that I care about your feelings when I apologize. I want you to understand that I didn't mean to bring any harm to you, and from now on, I'll do things differently.'*

The Components of a Meaningful, Heartfelt Apology

An effective apology conveys *the three R's*—remorse, responsibility, and remedy—clearly and concisely:

So,

- There needs to be an expression of *remorse* for being responsible for the trouble, harm, or destruction. Included is an indication of empathy for the other person, demonstrating that you recognize the hurt your actions or inaction caused them.

- There must be *an admission of guilt* regarding your deeds. This entails not pointing fingers at others or offering justifications for transgressions. It must be evident that you accept total accountability for your acts or inaction to make your apology meaningful.

- There needs to be *a declaration of your intent to do something to make things right*. Even though you cannot change the past, you can take all reasonable steps to make amends for the hurt you have caused. Therefore, a sincere apology must also include a promise to make amends in some way, to offer to aid the other individual or to take steps to ensure that the behavior won't happen again. For example, if you experienced physical or mental abuse as a child, you can promise to enroll in counseling or a support system to address your psychiatric issues. This is a remedy to help ensure you do not harm/abuse someone else again, be it your kids, partner, or coworkers. You could also offer to cover the cost of your victim's rehabilitation or give your money or time to charities supporting those affected by abuse.

This latter point is closely related to the next stage in making amends – developing a solid plan to learn from your mistakes and move past them and your guilt.

So, let's find out what it entails!

Chapter 5: Develop a Solid Plan to Address Your Mistakes & Move Past Them

The second part of making amends to eliminate your guilt is to go right ahead and develop a solid plan to address your mistakes, so you do not repeat them and thus feel even more guilt and shame moving forward.

Making mistakes is inevitable in life. Nobody has ever succeeded at that, and no one ever will. Regardless of your actions and measures, there is no way to prevent them and lead a mistake-free life.

Regarding mistakes, it is essential to understand that how you respond after making a mistake is more important (far more so) than the mistake itself or its scale.

Most successful people will tell you that success is almost always achieved through making mistakes and learning from failure. The majority, if not the entirety, of your mistakes, can serve as fantastic teaching moments. The same is valid for achieving success regarding eliminating your guilt and shame. Once you reframe your view on mistakes and address them promptly, so they do not recur, progress will swiftly follow.

Of course,

You will make mistakes and wrong people until your death and feel guilty because you are a decent person with a conscience.

But by addressing them and ensuring you do not repeat the same mistake twice, you will conquer your guilt and shame and prevent them from bogging your life down.

Steps to Follow

Here is how to address your mistakes so you can move past them and, in so doing, free yourself from the shackles of guilt and shame:

1) Acknowledge Your Mistakes

Admitting when you have erred is the very first step toward progress.

So, please don't attempt to hide, deny, or ignore it. Doing this will worsen the situation, put you under more stress, and sometimes hurt your reputation.

What should you do then?

Apologize if you feel the need to do so.

Think about the biggest mistake you have ever made.

Does anybody remember it anymore?

And,

Did it teach you anything new?

Ownership and honesty are brave, admirable traits and actions. Your grace and bravery in acknowledging mistakes and making amends will be remembered more than the mistakes or carelessness. And what's more, you will no longer feel so guilty and ashamed.

2) Reframe and Assess Your Mistake

The second step in learning is to alter your perspective on mistakes and wrongs. Make a concerted effort to remove yourself from your particular situation by addressing it head-on and reframing and analyzing it to improve your resilience, enabling you to view the broader picture. Both your professional and personal growth will benefit from this.

Ask yourself these questions in your bid to reframe and analyze your mistake and reason for your guilt:

- What exactly was it that I was attempting to do here?

- What happened?

- What went wrong, and when did it go wrong?

- Why did things go wrong?

The answers contain applicable life lessons and tips on avoiding making the same mistakes again and feeling guilty in the present and future.

3) Ask Yourself (and answer) some Hard Questions

Self-reflection is challenging, but it is essential if you are going to win the war against guilt and shame. Like ownership, not knowing what you did prevents you from making practical changes in your future interactions and actions, conquering your guilt, and preventing future guilt and shame rooted in the same thing.

Therefore, consider the events that led to your mistake, including any other errors you may have made.

4) Put all the Lessons You Learn from Your Mistakes into Practice

Though healthy at its core, introspection only goes so far, and you must follow it with actions to be effective.

So, apply the lessons you've learned from your mistakes to help stop you from being ashamed and guilty. That can entail improving communication skills, time management, or attention-to-detail tactics.

And remember,

Practice, indeed, does make perfect. The faster you improve, the more regularly you exercise your body and mind to act and think in a particular way. And in so doing, you will undercut your guilt and shame since it will have no anchor to get tethered to anymore and diminish chances of feeling guilty and ashamed in the future owing to the same mistake.

5) Review the Progress that You Make

Set aside time to analyze your accomplishments and *enlist the help of a dependable relative*, friend, or coworker to be your accountability partner.

Why?

There are two effective methods for keeping track of your progress and ensuring you do not make the same mistake and feel guilty and ashamed about it moving forward.

Your accountability partner can provide an objective viewpoint and typically a more transparent, uplifting opinion regarding your personal growth and development. This person can motivate you along the journey and aid you in staying on the right path and not making the same blunders.

6) Understand that it is indeed Okay for You to Feel/be Vulnerable

We often grapple with discouragement and vulnerability when we make mistakes and feel guilty about them; this is perfectly acceptable and normal.

But only when you are prepared to be receptive to these emotions can you advance and support others in doing the same, as well as truly put yourself in a position to master your guilt and shame.

7) Remember that Mistakes are Inevitable

We've said it multiple times and will repeat it – you will make mistakes and hurt people repeatedly; this is inevitable.

So what can you do?

You can only try your hardest, ask for assistance when necessary, be genuinely remorseful, and show support for those you've wronged when you inevitably blunder.

Viewing your mistakes as opportunities to learn and not as hooks to hang toxic guilt and shame onto is crucial.

We won't romanticize things; we can't afford to.

Life is hard, just as much as it's fantastic. There will be highs after lows, and things will go wrong and improve over time. You'll blunder and mess up.

But it's infinitely better to do everything possible to make amends and learn from your situation instead of crushing yourself with endless guilt and shame.

How?

✓ **_Try reading these encouraging quotes_** if you or somebody you know is having a bad day. You can count on them to make you smile and motivate you to compile what you've learned and keep going.

Here are some of the quotes:

✓ *"Yes, the past can be painful. But you can either ignore it or take valuable lessons from it."* Walt Disney

✓ *"Learn from each and every mistake you make because they are meant to enlighten you and push you to become more of the individual you are supposed to be, and not to saddle you with shame."* Oprah Winfrey

✓ *"The second biggest mistake you could make in life is to live in constant fear of doing anything wrong. The biggest one is killing yourself with shame every time you err."* Elbert Hubbard

✓ *"Nothing in our universe is flawless, which is one of the fundamental laws of nature. Without imperfections, you and I wouldn't be here."* Stephen Hawking

Chapter 6: Confront and Completely Revise Your Toxic Inner Voices

If you struggle with guilt and shame, chances are very high that you constantly grapple with a toxic inner voice that undermines you, undercuts your esteem, and ceaselessly puts you down.

This internal toxic voice is marked by strong, self-defeating, perennially negative messages that were probably first imparted to you as a youngster by your parents or other adult caregivers.

When you ignite your guilt and shame, usually in stressful situations or after making mistakes, your internal toxic voice becomes louder and bolder.

And,

If you were abused and shamed as a child, your toxic inner voice would likely be steady and more brutal to extinguish because abused children often idealize their primary caregiver, making it challenging to silence these toxic inner voices. The young child in you is dependent on your parents. As such, they cannot be wrong or evil. Therefore, you assume you must be the bad/evil one. This is the dynamic at play and likely one you may relate to if you look back on your childhood.

Years later, long after you have moved out of your parents' house and become a self-sufficient adult, these voices persist and worsen the toxic guilt and shame.

So, how do you confront and revise your inner toxic voice/dialogue?

Externalization is, by some distance, the most effective approach to modifying your internal dialogue.

When you speak or write about your self-talk – externalize it, so to speak – and you are thus able to really analyze and question the accuracy of these thoughts now that they're out in the open. That way, dispelling negative emotions and feelings such as anxiety, guilt, and shame becomes easy.

However, if your guilt and shame are rooted in traumas you may have suffered as a child, externalization alone may not be sufficient to modify and revise your inner dialogue completely, so it shifts from being toxic to being positive.

Here are several more steps that you need to take as well:

Steps to help Confront and Revise Your Toxic Inner Voice

- **Decide that You Have Had Enough!**

As humans, we all too often need to get to a point where we say to ourselves, *"I have had enough,"* before being able to make the changes we need to.

And,

Once you push yourself to the point where you feel you've had enough of your toxic inner voice and need to see a difference, you can confront it with purpose and boldness.

Beliefs and changes are often formed and activated during spells of intense emotion, such as anger. As such, the best way to trigger permanent change is to attach a fierce feeling to your problem (in this case, your guilt and the toxic inner voice accompanying it) and use it to spur you forward.

And yes; it's okay to be angry; not with yourself, but rather with your inner toxic voice's constant negativity and demeaning nature. You can then use your anger to motivate you to confront and change your unhealthy inner voice.

- **Acknowledge What Your Role Is, In Anything/Everything that Happens to You**

If you've made a mistake and harmed someone and honestly know it to be your fault, you must take responsibility and not give excuses or play the victim card. Especially with the latter, we often play the victim because it makes us feel better about ourselves. However, doing this solves nothing but only exacerbates the issue and fans the flames of guilt and shame.

Therefore,

The only way to truly take the fight against your guilt and shame is to *be completely honest with yourself.* Train yourself to acknowledge your role in every situation you are involved in and everything that happens to you. And always be brutally honest with yourself.

As you get older, become more conscious and aware that some areas of your day-to-day lives are not working out as they should; you are responsible for modifying your views and perceptions of the same and mapping out your future paths.

And even when it appears that something is somebody else's fault, as long as the situation/circumstance involves you, you can determine how it affects you moving forward and whether there is any accountability you need to take regarding the same.

So, always establish your role in something that may be causing you to feel guilty.

- **Challenge the Limiting Beliefs You May Have**

Your beliefs shape your experiences.

These beliefs, however, are not always as accurate or even authentic as you may believe. What you believe to be factual may indeed only be rooted in factoids.

So,

Try this simple exercise to challenge any limiting beliefs you have:

Start by listing a few of the limiting beliefs you have on a napkin or paper. Write down your justifications for every opinion, then get answers to these questions:

✓ Are there any personal experiences that might conflict with my beliefs in one way or another?

✓ What proof do I have that what I think is true is true?

✓ Am I falling into a mental trap, such as catastrophizing or an all-or-nothing outlook?

✓ What advice would I give a friend with the same beliefs and way of thinking?

✓ Am I conflating a belief/sentiment with an accurate statement?

✓ Am I more likely to base my judgment on the truth rather than how I feel or think to be true?

You'll realize very quickly that most of your self-limiting beliefs will fall apart under your scrutiny and line of questioning, which will mean that your toxic inner voice has no fuel to keep running on.

- ## Use Gratitude to Break Away from Your Old Belief System

That's right; be genuinely grateful that your restrictive beliefs were at least doing their best to preserve and protect you.

But how so, you may ask?

Well, we are hardwired as a species to minimize unnecessary risks to preserve our evolution better. Self-limiting beliefs serve this purpose – they prevent us from taking too many risks, thus ensuring some stability.

However, we do not need self-limiting beliefs in this day and age like our ancestors did; in fact, they do more harm than good.

Nevertheless, be grateful for them.

Although it may seem counterintuitive, being grateful makes it simpler to shake off outdated beliefs and develop new, useful ones.

That doesn't imply that you approve of or desire that your subconscious holds onto these outdated notions. It simply means that you accept the reality that these beliefs were there and were influential in self-preservation and that you're now prepared to update them.

Therefore, acknowledge and be grateful but also make it clear to yourself that their time is up and that you need something completely different moving forward to grow and evolve.

How?

Try this simple exercise:

- ✓ List your old, restrictive, and limiting beliefs, and then write an appreciation note describing how they have benefited you previously.

- ✓ Express your appreciation, gratitude, and desire to let it go now that its purpose is complete.

✓ Make it clear that each limiting belief you just listed is outlawed from being part of your belief system moving forward.

- **Change Your Story**

You must examine what happened and change any narrative you may have built around those events if you are to shed your outdated ideas and limiting beliefs and thus have an easier time revising your toxic inner voice.

Here is an example,

Think about the time, as a child, when your parents left the house in the morning for work, and you, as a child, perhaps thought, *"Oh no, they're abandoning me!"* You may even have thrown a tantrum for a while after they left.

Even though they told you they needed to go to work to help the family and even left a babysitter at home to take care of you at the time, you were just too young to grasp why they had to go and not spend the whole day with you playing and having fun.

What you thought back then about them leaving was not the case but a narrative you built up in your head. You know this for a fact right now, albeit you did not know it back then.

Therefore, it is imperative that, as an adult, you examine your situation to see if your beliefs and perspective are rooted in fact or a narrative.

Try this simple exercise:

Start **_taking an unbiased view of what has happened in your life_**.

Ask yourself these questions:

- ✓ What indeed took place?

- ✓ What impact did it have on the other person's life?

- ✓ Did you intend to hurt them, or was it just something you did to benefit yourself without considering whether it was detrimental to others?

These questions will help you determine if your guilt is founded or comes from a narrative you've constructed for yourself.

Next, you must acknowledge your self-hatred's "safety" and start your self-love journey.

Chapter 7: Acknowledge The "Safety" of Self-Hatred & Get Started on Your Self-Love Journey

Do you remember how in the previous chapter, we pointed to your self-limiting beliefs being tools of self-preservation, albeit outdated and more damaging than helpful?

The same is the case with self-hatred. You may not know it, but self-hatred is, in fact, a self-help mechanism.

But let's back up for a second,

Usually, everything you do has a purpose. And practicing self-hate is no different.

Self-loathing protects and preserves you, in a sense.

If you hate yourself for the wrongs that others may have done to you as a child, for example, you put yourself in a position where you redirect your hate from them to yourself and thus do not get enraged every time you think about them. Placing the blame on yourself instead of those who harmed you and hating yourself keeps you in a "safe" bubble where you are not constantly angry at them and circumstances you have no control over.

Self-hate, in this regard, may have served as a means of survival. You merely wanted to keep yourself safe.

The problem is that self-hate is not a viable solution to anything. And what is more, nothing fans the flames of guilt and shame as self-hate does.

It may provide short-term relief, but long-term improvements are unfeasible. Additionally, it makes it impossible to heal from your trauma, further poisoning your mental wellness and making your life more miserable.

You must overcome your self-hatred and develop self-love to grow, heal from your trauma, and extinguish your guilt and shame for good.

But how?

How to get over Your Self-hatred

Here is how to get over your self-hatred:

1. Let all Your Past Mistakes and Regrets Go

To truly love yourself, you must completely ignore the 'what-ifs' that dominate your thoughts.

Why?

✓ Dwelling on your past is not a good habit because no change will come from it, regardless of how much energy you spend living on it. You only have power over your choices in the here and now.

✓ Focusing on your past will only lead to a stream of negative thoughts which highlight your shortcomings instead of the (many) positive qualities you possess.

Therefore, staying as far away from negativity is essential to love yourself. When there is negativity and pessimism in your life, you are more likely than not to fixate on it, which will automatically cause you not to love yourself enough.

2. Never Compare Yourself to Other People

Eliminating your negative self-talk is necessary if you want to know how to love yourself truly.

And,

The simplest way to achieve this is to stop comparing yourself to others. And even though it is challenging to accomplish, especially in settings such as schools and workplaces where promotions and grading are virtually a game of politics, understand that your value is unaffected by the outside circumstances or what happens to/with others.

Practice self-compassion when others have good fortune, at least for your mental well-being. And even if you wind up on the less-desirable end of things, strive to be grateful and happy for others.

As they say, you'll have your chance; there is enough for us all.

Perhaps not in that particular setting, but in the end, we all get what we want if we keep at it. You deserve your fair share of respect, and comparing yourself to others leads to a lack of respect and regard for yourself and others.

And,

If you think about it, there's no reason to make someone else's success about yourself.

3. Embrace Contentment

Probably, you feel that you've not achieved the work and career goals you had for this particular period in your life or have not developed into the person you envisioned.

However, it's crucial to avoid dwelling on those things that you wish you could change and alter in the present; in the same way, you shouldn't dwell on mistakes and regrets from the past.

While some pressure is healthy, this way of thinking puts far too much stress and strain on you to fix everything immediately.

So what's the best thing to do?

Embrace who you are while also acknowledging you could (and should) work on doing and being better. Accepting the person you are in this particular season of your life without imposing undue pressure and strain on yourself is the first step in truly loving yourself. The more you worry that you aren't where you want to be, the more you'll overthink anything and everything in and around your life, making you feel worse again.

That is the only approach to take.

4. Make Sure to Surround Yourself with Positive People

Regarding self-love, the people you choose to be in your life are crucial. Once you surround yourself with people who are upbeat, supportive, and dreamers, their energy will start to rub off and transfer to you, and before long, you'll find yourself loving and appreciating yourself all the more.

Self-love is just about feeling great about yourself and your potential and having faith and confidence in your personal qualities regardless of your present state. That is why being positive and accepting of yourself as you are is typically the key to practicing self-love, even when you feel you can and should be doing better.

5. Focus on Positive Emotions

You must learn to love yourself.

How though?

- ✓ You can substitute your negative thoughts for positive ones.

- ✓ When things don't turn out the way you had hoped, be kind and compassionate to yourself.

- ✓ Engage in pleasant activities as much as possible, such as dancing as you cook or treating yourself to a night out occasionally.

- ✓ Read uplifting material, show unwavering affection to yourself at every chance, and allow happiness to seep into your life.

- ✓ You can also perform everyday acts of kindness for others for the same effect.

✓ Or you can write a brief love letter to yourself as a constant reminder of your value.

✓ If you are dissatisfied with something, be graceful about it and do your best to get over it so that you may steer your life in a better, more progressive direction.

6. Accept Yourself as You Are

Self-acceptance is the first step to self-love.

Your mistakes do not define who you are as a person. No one is perfect, not even the most well-put-together person you know. You cannot, therefore, constantly criticize yourself because you made a mistake.

However, how you respond to them and your actions once you've learned from them genuinely count.

So, how do you practice self-acceptance?

- ✓ Lead by example.

- ✓ Put an end to the pessimistic ideas that invade your mind.

- ✓ Don't let self-deception that you aren't good enough influence you.

- ✓ Stop latching onto excuses, take care of yourself, and put your health first.

- ✓ Accept responsibility for your words and actions, but also afford yourself forgiveness and compassion.

There's no need to live a life filled with guilt. Ultimately, your poor decisions and mistakes will help you become a better person, and you will be able to process happiness more quickly the quicker you internalize this.

Chapter 8: Transmute Your Shame and Guilt into Perennial Gratitude

We've discussed a lot about making mistakes, feeling guilty about errors and wrongs, and permitting yourself to make mistakes instead of letting yourself deteriorate into toxic guilt and shame.

We've also established beyond all reasonable doubt that mistakes are inevitable. That you will hurt other people and be in the center of mishaps as long as you live, and your response to your mistakes and the lessons you allow yourself to learn are essential.

Basically, we've thoroughly covered mistake/mishap-founded guilt and rewired your mind to undercut it.

But,

What about the guilt of being alright or prosperous while others are not so lucky?

What about survivor's guilt? What about the thriver's guilt?

This guide would not be complete if it did not show you how to deal with them, especially now that we've just come out of a global pandemic that ruined and took lives, wiped off jobs, and tilted the world socially and financially.

After the Corona Virus pandemic, many of us are in constant battle with survivor's and thriver's guilt. Some of us feel guilty that we made out relatively unharmed, while others still have medical problems or have lost their lives. We may feel guilty because we kept our jobs and our finances remained relatively unchanged, while some folks we know and love were not so lucky and perhaps even lost their homes in addition to losing their family and friends.

The survivor's and thriver's guilt are genuine and more prevalent than you might think.

Let's examine them before showing you how to deal with this kind of guilt.

Survivor's Guilt Versus Thriver's Guilt

Although it can make you feel awful, and we've touched on this already, guilt isn't always bad. It is a manifestation of self-awareness.

For instance, guilt can encourage self-reflection and behavioral modification when you have wronged and harmed others, be it intentionally or unintentionally. However, on occasion, guilt sentiments develop for unfair reasons.

Think about the case of survivor's guilt. ***The survivor's guilt** develops when you are unaffected by a scenario that causes harm to others*. For instance, most folks who survive mass tragedies like natural disasters grapple with survivor's remorse. It is also present in those who manage not to catch an illness or recover from it but know of others who aren't as fortunate.

On the other hand, there is no recognized definition of **thriver's guilt** compared to survivor's guilt. So, we will define it as *the sentiments of guilt which may appear when you prosper despite or perhaps even as a result of a circumstance/situation/catastrophe that has harmed or maybe devastated others.*

So, what can you do, or what should you do, if you are grappling with survivor's or thriver's guilt right now?

How to Deal with Survivor's and Thriver's Guilt

- **Be Grateful and Constantly Express Your Gratitude for Other**

If you are struggling with survivor's or thriver's guilt, understand that you aren't the only one with this problem.

For example, some people who work in particular sectors, professions, and industries managed to prosper despite and perhaps even as a result of the Covid 19 pandemic. As more and more activities shifted to an online platform, there was an increase in demand for specialists in e-learning and online-based business. As more people scrambled to construct new homes and refurbish old ones, so they were better suited for remote work, other industries, such as the building business, also prospered. Naturally, companies that provided services to industries directly linked to preventing and curing the Covid pandemic also benefited.

Overall, millions (yes, millions) of people saw a boom in their enterprises during the epidemic rather than a bust. And the Covid pandemic is just one example we are using here because all of us are familiar with it and have been affected by it to some degree.

Take some time to acknowledge your privilege and express gratitude if you were lucky enough to land a job in any of these fields, saw your business survive and even thrive through it, or some other difficult period.

Additionally, express your gratitude to all your team/enterprise/venture members during the Covid 19 pandemic.

It's a nice thing to express gratitude to your colleagues. According to research, being grateful has a favorable effect on employees' productivity and well-being. In this regard, voice/show your gratitude to other people. Appreciating what you've got is a potent way to transmute your survivor's or thriver's guilt into something which will benefit you, your entire team, and your company for years and years to come.

- **Give Back to the Community**

Consider contributing to the community in addition to expressing your thanks.

Look into practical ways to aid others in rebounding in their lives if your enterprise/career thrived despite or due to the Covid pandemic or some other difficult season.

Even away from catastrophes and difficult seasons, if you have been lucky to enjoy considerable success while your childhood friends are struggling, see if you can do anything to help them get on their feet.

For instance,

✓ Can you introduce additional positions in your enterprise to assist laid-off employees in rejoining the workforce?

✓ Are you equipped with the resources to retrain employees who lost their jobs in other industries?

✓ Can you use the resources at your disposal to address other urgent needs in your neighborhood, such as housing or food insecurity?

You might not have had the time or finances to volunteer or participate in charitable activities before the epidemic or some other difficult season that saw you thrive. But instead of feeling guilty if you prospered when others were experiencing difficulties, reevaluate your capacity to contribute. That is the best way to transmute your guilt into gratitude.

We also dipped into Quora, the global discussion forum, for more good perspectives that folks who've struggled with guilt may have concerning transmuting guilt and shame into gratitude.

We've outlined them below.

Note: None of these people are celebrities or famous; they're just people with typical lives who've struggled with guilt and learned some valuable lessons.

1. *Meena – Los Angeles, California*

"I felt guilty for not taking better care of my elderly parents and parents-in-law.

So, how did I deal with this guilt?

I decided to do something about it. For starters, I have made sure the number of my visits and conversations with them has tripled, in addition to other things. I make sure to thank them for all of my accomplishments because, without their affection and guidance during my formative years, I wouldn't have been able to pursue my work in a fulfilling way.

Friends, remember that our parents rarely tell us that they would like more quality time with you; it is up to us to give it to them so that they may enjoy it in their later years. We should also show them our gratitude as often as we can. It will change everything, both for them and for us."

2. Abshilasha Dabral – New Delhi, India

He said, "If you are guilty of something you did, you must ask the individual you harmed for forgiveness. If this isn't the case, however, and you're feeling guilty for something that was your fault, you must try your hardest to stop thinking about it because you're not at fault.

Instead, be grateful that you made it out alright and see if you can extend this gratitude to those who were not as lucky by trying to help them."

3. Keren Joy – Dublin, Ireland

(Keren Joy takes a religious stance on guilt and changing your guilt into gratitude from a spiritual perspective.)

"I think it depends on what exactly you are feeling guilty about. We occasionally feel wrong about things that are beyond our control.

There are ways to flip your shame into appreciation if you're feeling guilty about a mistake or transgression. The Bible states that death is the wage of sin. Sin carries a price that must be paid. Jesus came to bear this terrible price for our sins, sparing you from dying and going to hell and allowing you to enjoy eternal life in heaven instead. Therefore, repent and confess your guilt to God.

Acknowledge that Jesus did indeed die for you. He endured the suffering so you wouldn't have to. According to the Bible, we are set free when we ask God to forgive us and acknowledge that Jesus has already paid the ultimate penalty for our sins on the cross. He has forgotten about our transgressions. There is no longer any condemnation. As such, there is no reason to continue feeling guilty, my friend. Does that not transform your shame into gratitude? Think about it."

Conclusion

Guilt is not a bad thing – at least natural guilt isn't. But if you allow it to thicken and become murky so that it eventually turns into toxic guilt and shame, then it becomes an awful thing that could (and likely will) prove quite debilitating for you.

Therefore, you must use all the tips and strategies this guide outlines to help you battle guilt and shame. Seek to understand your guilt first, trace it down to its roots and then make the necessary amends, both with yourself and others, and execute the essential cognitive revisions so you can rewire your mind to perceive guilt differently.

You can eliminate guilt and shame in no time if you're vigilant and consistent.

PS: I'd like your feedback. If you are happy with this book, please leave a review on Amazon.

Please leave a review for this book on Amazon by visiting the page below:

https://amzn.to/2VMR5qr

Printed in Great Britain
by Amazon

40815009R00066